D0928090

ALEX KUSKOWSKI

Consulting Editor, Diane Craig, M.A./Reading Specialist

Super Sandcastle

An Imprint of Abdo Publishing
abdopublishing.com

abdopublishing.com

Published by Abdo Publishing, a division of ABDO, PO Box 398166, Minneapolis, Minnesota 55439. 

Printed in the United States of America, North Mankato, Minnesota
102015
012016

THIS BOOK CONTAINS RECYCLED MATERIALS

Editor: Liz Salzmann
Content Developer: Nancy Tuminelly
Cover and Interior Design and Production: Mighty Media, Inc.
Photo Credits: Mighty Media, Inc. and Shutterstock

The following manufacturers/names appearing in this book are trademarks: Arm & Hammer®, Brer Rabbit®, C&H®, Calumet®, Duncan Hines®, Market Pantry™, McCormick®, Proctor Silex®, Pyrex®, Rolo®

**Library of Congress Cataloging-in-Publication Data**
Kuskowski, Alex, author.
Super simple specialty cookies : easy cookie recipes for kids! / Alex Kuskowski.
pages cm. -- (Super simple cookies)
ISBN 978-1-62403-951-5
1. Cookies--Juvenile literature. 2. Baking--Juvenile literature. I. Title.
TX772.K7785 2016
641.86'54--dc23
2015020626

Super SandCastle™ books are created by a team of professional educators, reading specialists, and content developers around five essential components—phonemic awareness, phonics, vocabulary, text comprehension, and fluency—to assist young readers as they develop reading skills and strategies and increase their general knowledge. All books are written, reviewed, and leveled for guided reading and early reading intervention programs for use in shared, guided, and independent reading and writing activities to support a balanced approach to literacy instruction.

## TO ADULT HELPERS

Help your child learn to cook! Cooking lets children practice math and science. It teaches kids about responsibility and boosts their confidence. Plus they get to make some great food!

Before getting started, set ground rules for using the kitchen, cooking tools, and ingredients. There should always be adult supervision when use of a sharp tool, oven, or stove is required. Be aware of the symbols below that indicate when special care is necessary.

So, put on your apron and get ready to cheer on your new chef!

## SYMBOLS

### Hot!

This recipe requires the use of a stove or oven. You will need adult supervision and assistance.

### Sharp!

This recipe includes the use of a sharp utensil such as a knife or grater. Ask an adult to help out.

### Nuts!

This recipe includes nuts. Find out whether anyone you are serving has a nut allergy.

# CONTENTS


| | |
|---|---|
| Creative Specialty Cookies | 4 |
| Cooking Basics | 6 |
| Measuring Ingredients | 8 |
| Did You Know This = That? | 9 |
| Cooking Terms | 10 |
| Kitchen Utensils | 12 |
| Ingredients | 14 |
| Potato Chip Cookies | 16 |
| Delicious Jammy Tarts | 18 |
| Sweet Pretzel Treats | 20 |
| Sprinkle Sandwiches | 22 |
| Buttery Tea Cakes | 24 |
| Stained Glass Cookies | 26 |
| Red Velvet Delights | 30 |
| Glossary | 32 |


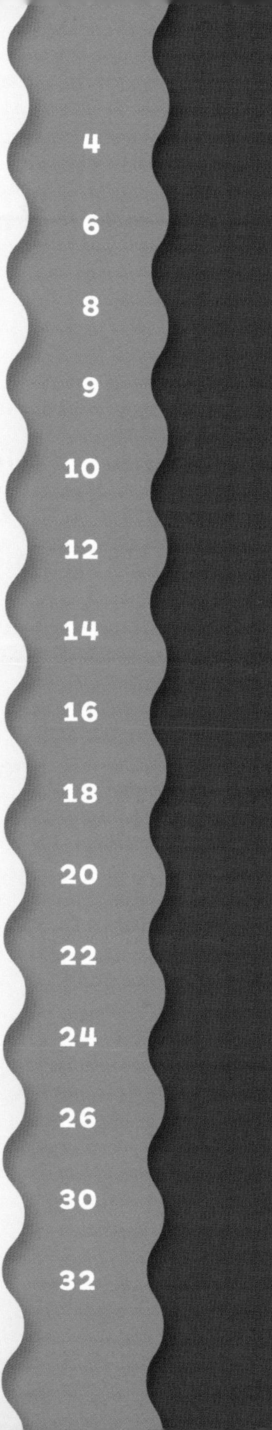

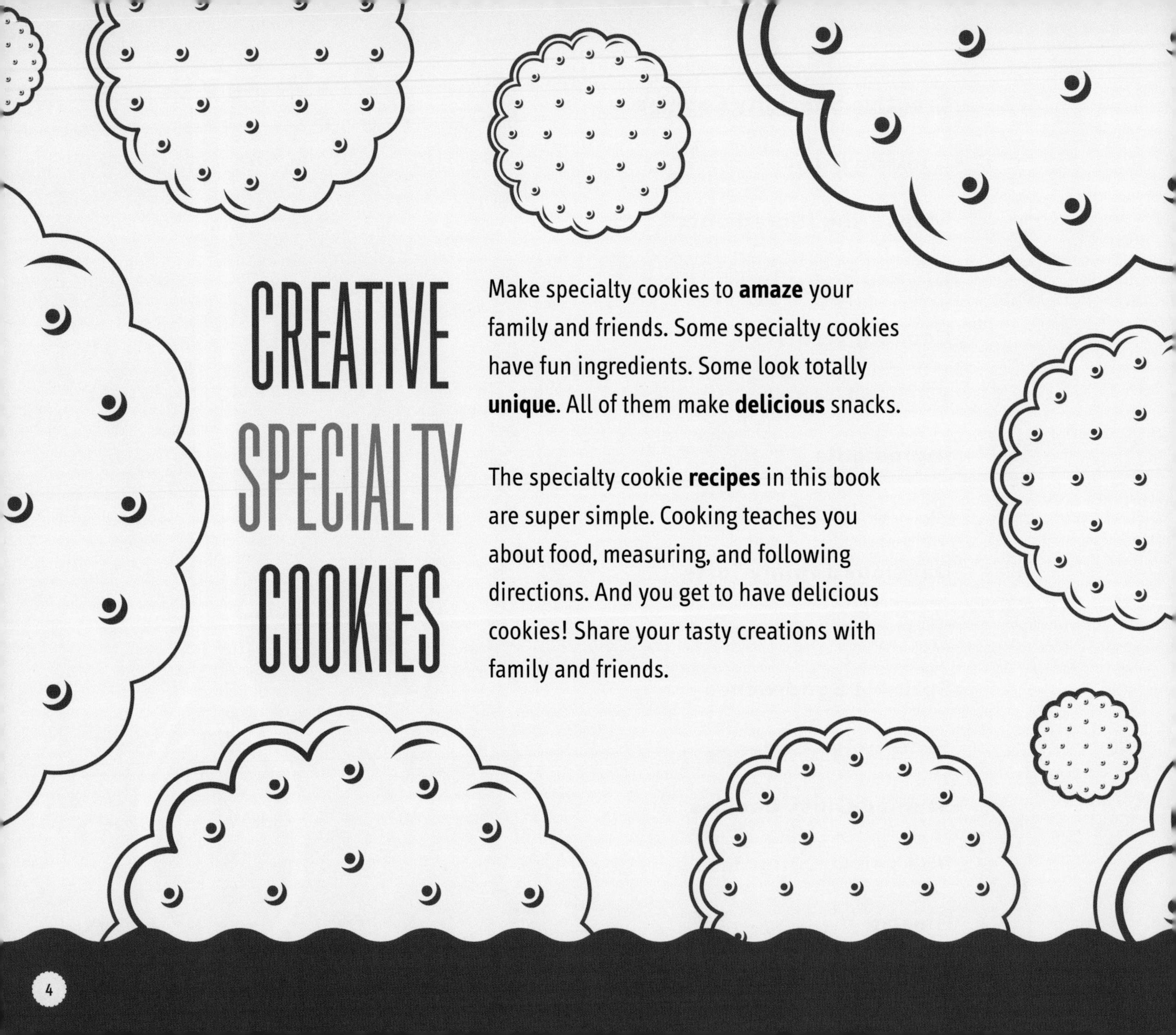

# CREATIVE SPECIALTY COOKIES

Make specialty cookies to **amaze** your family and friends. Some specialty cookies have fun ingredients. Some look totally **unique**. All of them make **delicious** snacks.

The specialty cookie **recipes** in this book are super simple. Cooking teaches you about food, measuring, and following directions. And you get to have delicious cookies! Share your tasty creations with family and friends.

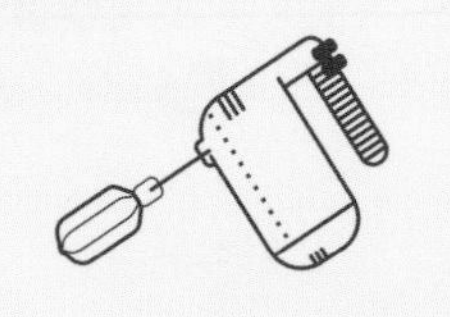
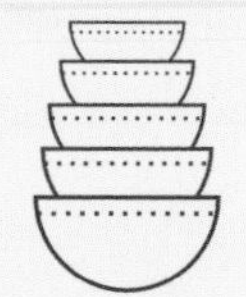

# COOKING BASICS

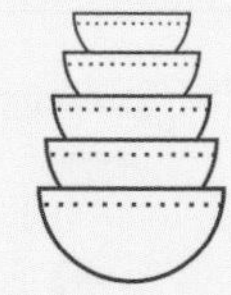
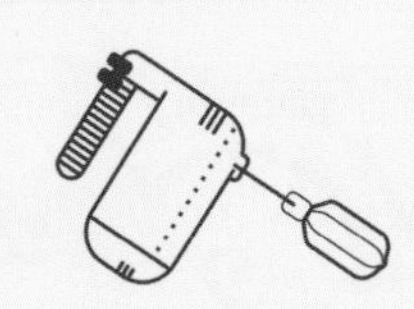

## Think Safety!

- Ask an adult to help you use a knife. Place things on a cutting board to cut them.
- Clean up spills right away.
- Keep things away from the edge of the table or **counter**.
- Ask an adult to help you use the oven.
- Ask for help if you cannot reach something.

## Using the Oven

- Preheat the oven while making the **recipe**.
- Use oven-safe dishes.
- Use pot holders or oven mitts to hold hot things.
- Do not touch the oven door. It can be very hot.
- Set a timer. Check the food and bake longer if needed.

## Before Baking

- Get **permission** from an adult.
- Wash your hands.
- Read the recipe at least once.
- Set out the ingredients and tools you will need.
- Keep a **towel** close by for cleaning up spills.

## When You're Done

- Let the cookies cool completely.
- Store the cookies in **containers**. Put a sheet of waxed paper in between the **layers** of cookies.
- Put all the ingredients and tools away.
- Wash all the dishes and **utensils**. Clean up your work space.

# MEASURING INGREDIENTS

## Wet Ingredients

Set a measuring cup on the **counter**. Add the liquid. Stop when it reaches the amount you need. Check the measurement from eye level.

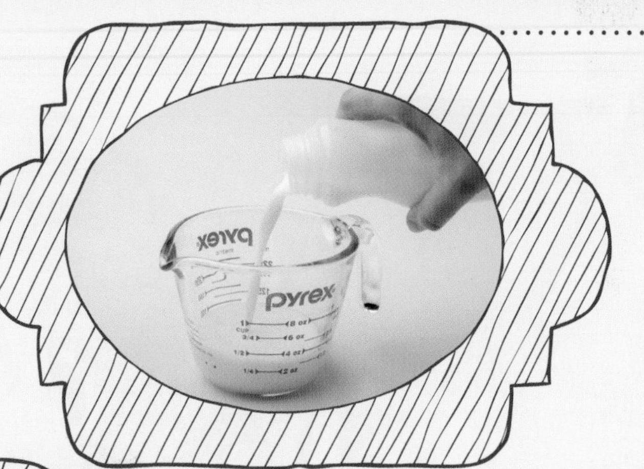

## Dry Ingredients

Dip the measuring cup or spoon into the dry ingredient. Fill it with a little more than you need. Use the back of a dinner knife to remove the extra.

## Moist Ingredients

Measure ingredients such as brown sugar and dried fruit differently. Press them down into the measuring cup.

# DID YOU KNOW THIS = THAT?

There are different ways to measure the same amount.

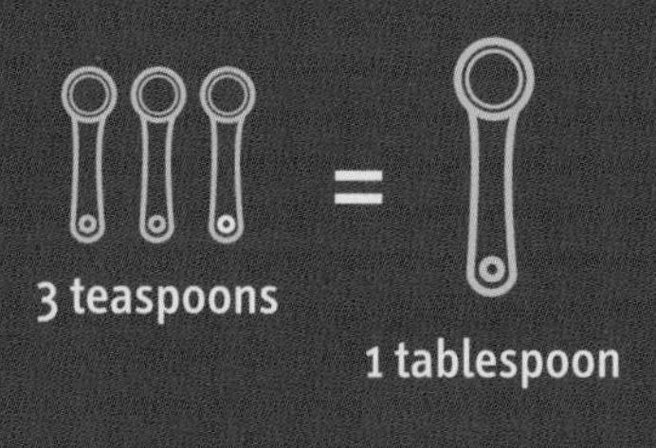

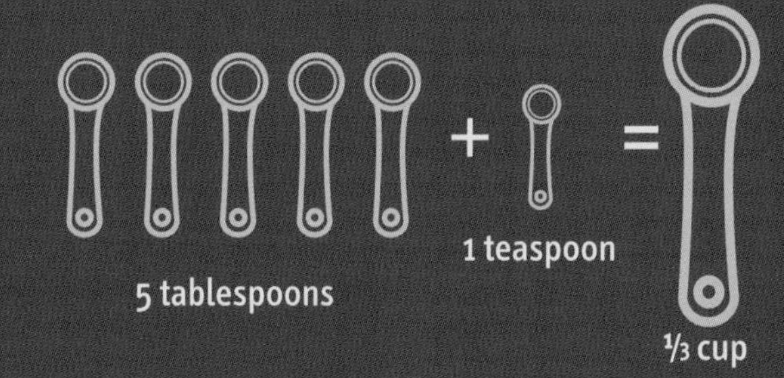

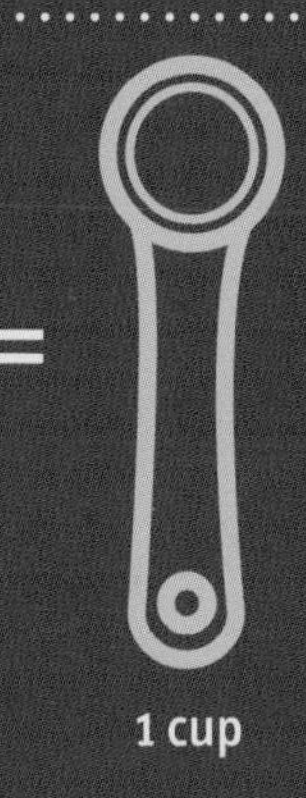


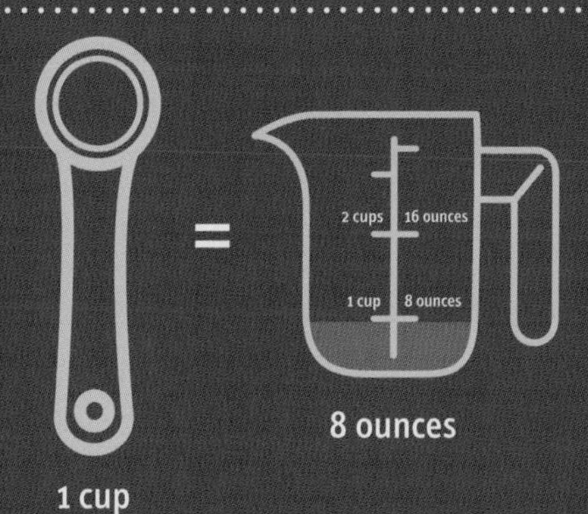


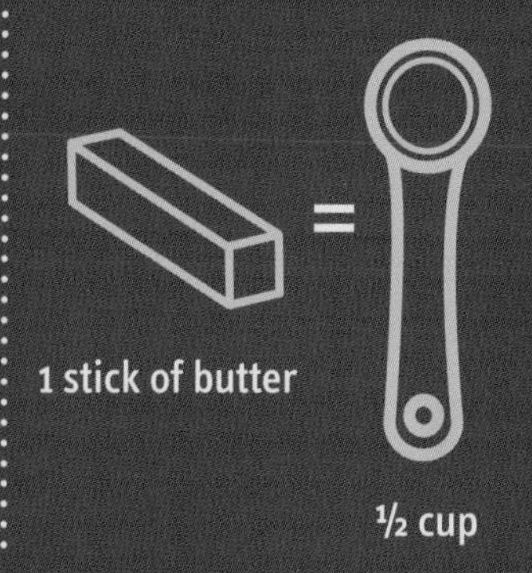

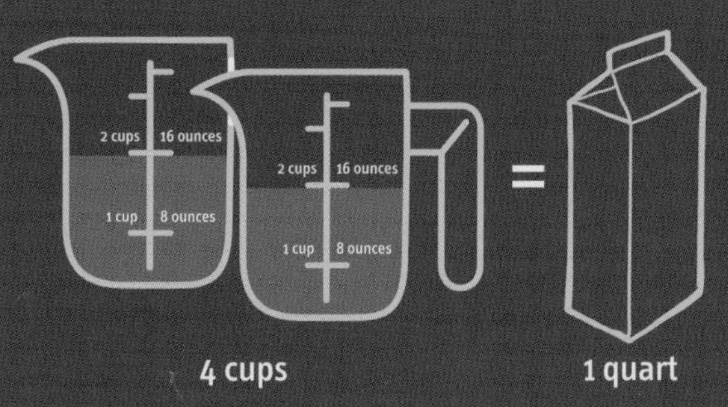

# COOKING TERMS

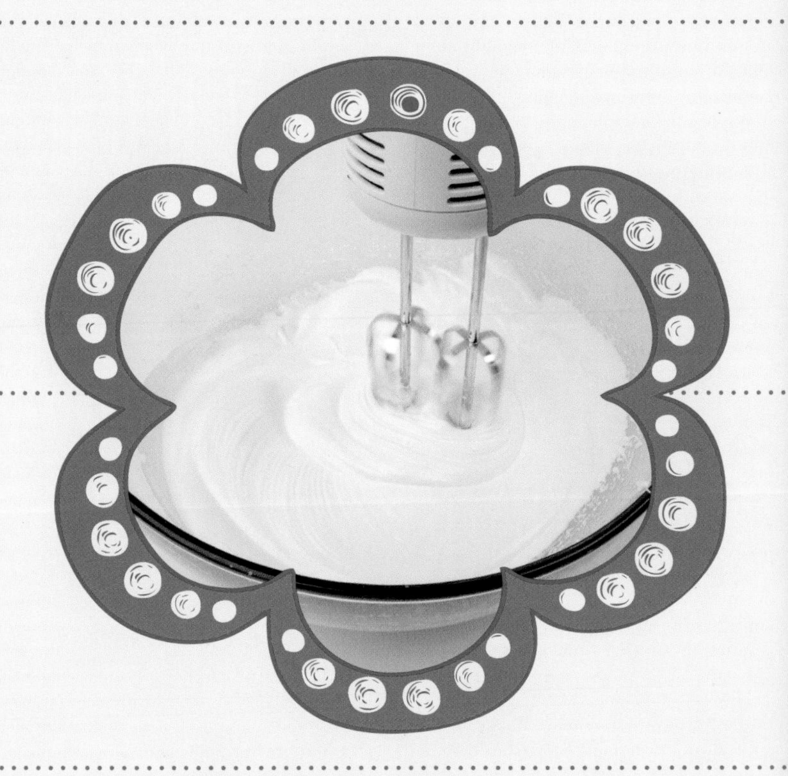

## CRUSH

Crush means to mash something into very small pieces.

## CREAM

Cream means to beat butter and sugar together until light and **fluffy**.

## STIR

Stir means to mix ingredients together, usually with a spoon or rubber spatula.

## SPREAD

Spread means to make a smooth **layer** with a spoon, knife, or rubber spatula.

# KITCHEN UTENSILS

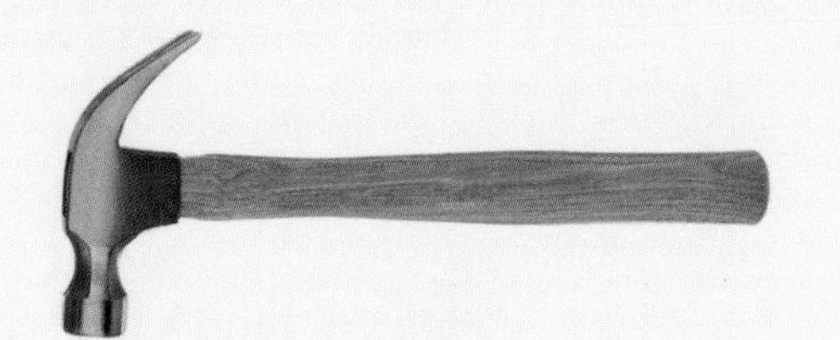

hammer

measuring spoons

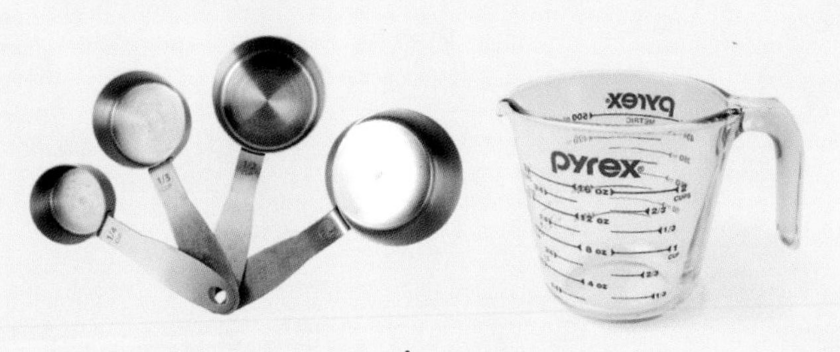


measuring cups

sharp knife

mixing bowls

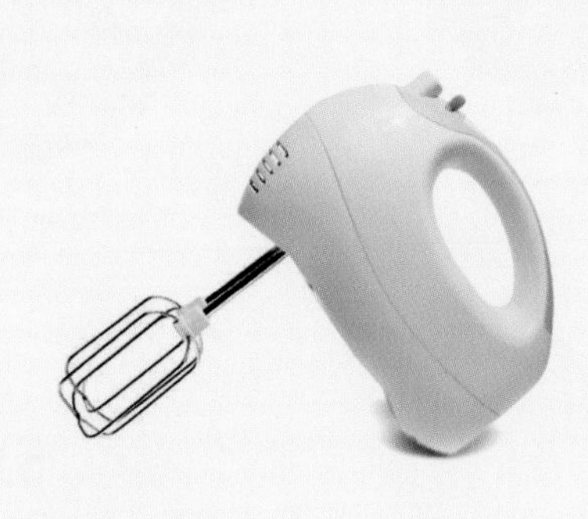

electric mixer

cutting board

rolling pin

mixing spoon

plastic zipper bags

cookie cutters

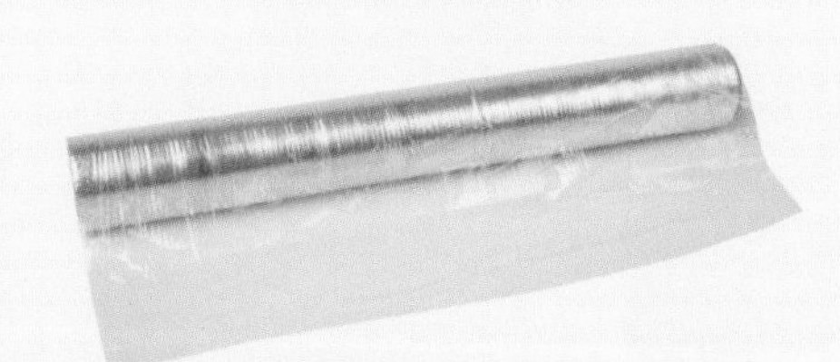

plastic wrap

pot holders

drinking glass

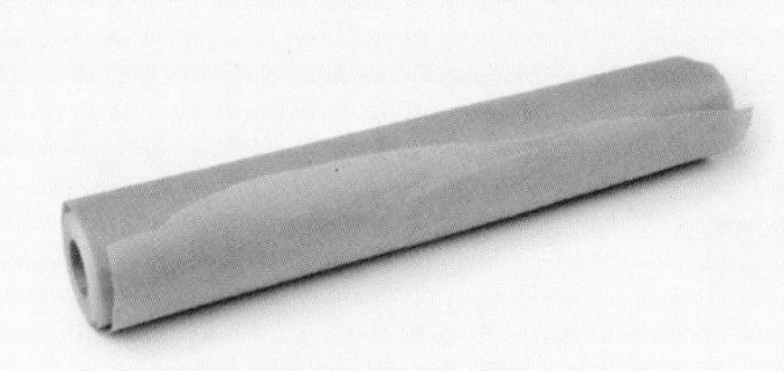

parchment paper

spatula

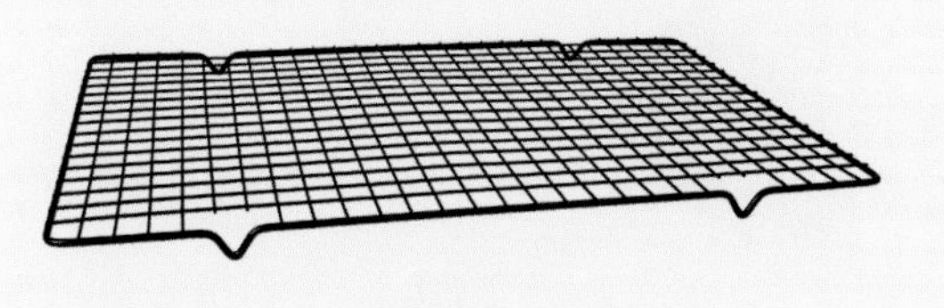

cooling rack

baking sheet

# INGREDIENTS

all-purpose flour

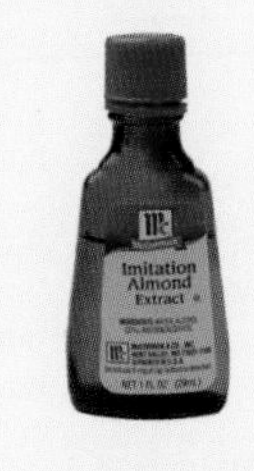

almond extract

baking powder

baking soda

brown sugar

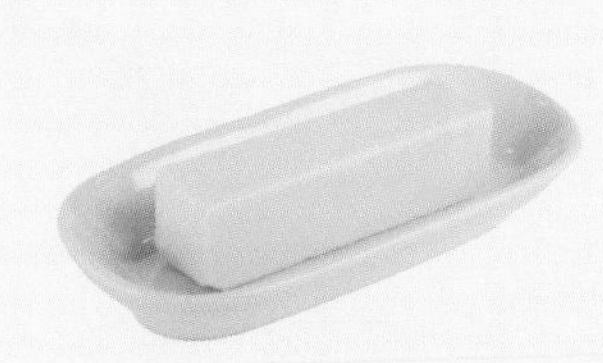
butter

butterscotch chips

chocolate-covered peanuts

chopped walnuts

cocoa powder

colored sprinkles

eggs

ground cinnamon

ground ginger

hard candy
marmalade
milk
BRER RABBIT
Molasses
FULL FLAVOR
molasses
nutmeg
C&H
CANE SUGAR
Pure
CANE
SUGAR
POWDERED
powdered sugar
raspberry jam
Duncan Hines
NEW!
DECADENT
RED VELVET CUPCAKE
red velvet cake mix
Rolos
salt
salted potato chips
small pretzels
pure
vanilla
extract
vanilla extract
vegetable oil
white chocolate chips
white sugar

# potato chip cookies

MAKES 24 COOKIES

## INGREDIENTS

2¼ cups all-purpose flour
½ teaspoon salt
1 teaspoon baking soda
1 cup butter
¾ cup brown sugar
¾ cup white sugar
1 teaspoon vanilla extract
2 large eggs
¾ cup butterscotch chips
4 cups crushed salted potato chips

## TOOLS

baking sheets
parchment paper
measuring cups
measuring spoons
mixing bowls
mixing spoon
electric mixer
pot holders
spatula
cooling rack

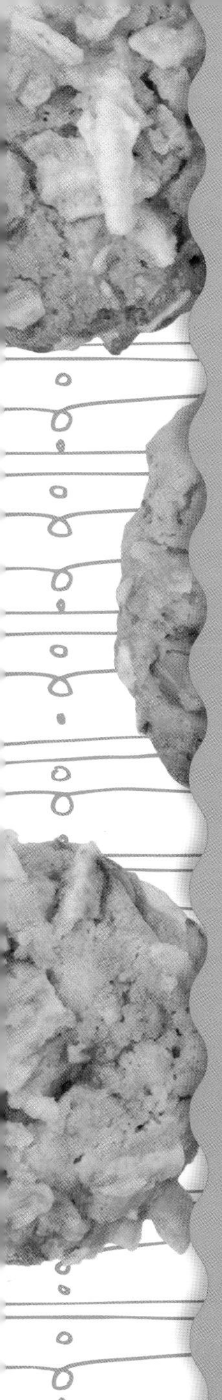

1. Preheat the oven to 350 degrees. Cover the baking sheets with parchment paper.
2. Put the flour, salt, and baking soda in a small bowl. Stir.
3. Cream the butter and both sugars in a large bowl. Mix in the vanilla and eggs with the electric mixer. Add the flour mixture to the sugar mixture. Mix well.
4. Add the butterscotch chips and 2 cups crushed potato chips. Stir.
5. Put the remaining crushed potato chips in a bowl. Roll the dough into 1-inch (2.5 cm) balls. Coat each ball with potato chips. Place the balls on the baking sheets.
6. Bake for 11 minutes or until they are golden brown. Put the cookies on a cooling rack.

delicious
jammy
tarts

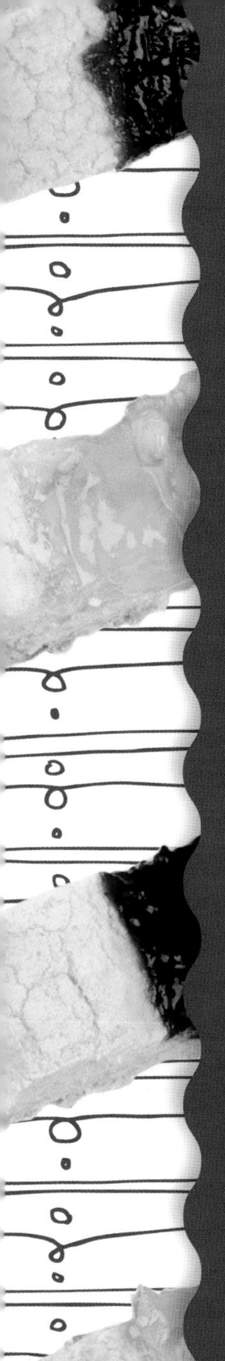

MAKES 20 COOKIES

## INGREDIENTS

- 2 cups all-purpose flour
- ¾ teaspoon salt
- ½ teaspoon baking powder
- ¾ cup butter
- ⅔ cup white sugar
- 1 large egg
- 1 teaspoon vanilla extract
- 1 teaspoon almond extract
- 2 tablespoons vegetable oil
- ½ cup marmalade
- ½ cup raspberry jam

## TOOLS

- baking sheet
- parchment paper
- measuring cups
- measuring spoons
- mixing bowls
- electric mixer
- mixing spoon
- pot holders
- sharp knife
- cutting board

1. Preheat the oven to 350 degrees. Cover the baking sheet with parchment paper.
2. Put the flour, salt, and baking powder in a medium bowl. Mix with an electric mixer.
3. Cream the butter and sugar in a large bowl. Mix in the egg, vanilla extract, almond extract, and oil. Add the flour mixture to the sugar mixture. Mix well.
4. **Divide** the dough in half. Roll each half into a log 2 inches (5 cm) wide and 10 inches (25 cm) long.
5. Put the logs on the baking sheet. Use the end of a mixing spoon to make an indent down the middle of the logs.
6. Fill one log with marmalade. Fill the other log with raspberry jam.
7. Bake the logs for 18 minutes. Take them out of the oven. Let them cool for 15 minutes. Cut the logs into 1-inch (2.5 cm) **slices**.

# sweet pretzel treats

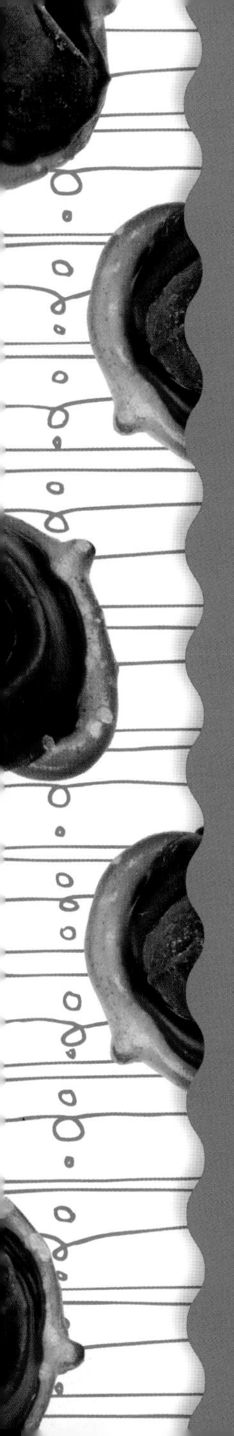

MAKES 30 COOKIES

## INGREDIENTS

2 cups small pretzels
1 package Rolos
1 cup chocolate-covered peanuts

## TOOLS

baking sheets
parchment paper
measuring cups
pot holders

1. Preheat the oven to 220 degrees. Cover the baking sheets with parchment paper.
2. Put the pretzels on the baking sheets. Space them ½ inch (1.3 cm) apart.
3. Put a Rolo on top of each pretzel. Bake for 3 minutes. Take them out of the oven.
4. Press a chocolate-covered peanut on top of each Rolo. Refrigerate for 20 minutes.

# sprinkle sandwiches

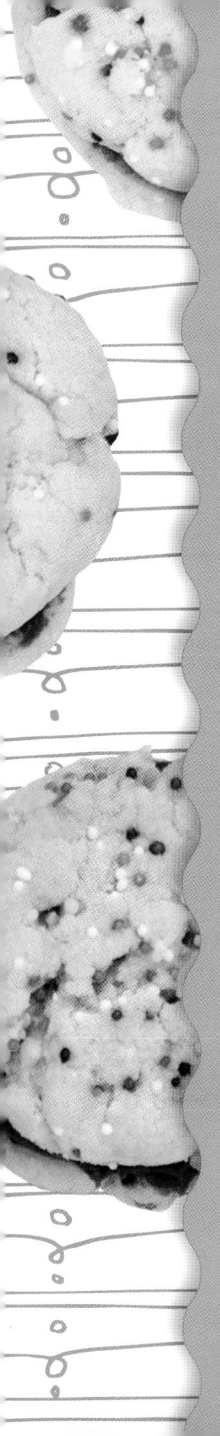

MAKES 12 SANDWICHES

## INGREDIENTS

COOKIES

½ cup butter
¾ cup white sugar
1 egg
1 teaspoon vanilla extract
1¾ cup all-purpose flour
½ teaspoon salt
1 teaspoon baking powder
¾ cup colored sprinkles

FROSTING

½ cup butter
1½ cups powdered sugar
¼ cup cocoa powder
¼ teaspoon salt
1 teaspoon vanilla extract
2 tablespoons milk

## TOOLS

baking sheets
parchment paper
measuring cups
measuring spoons
mixing bowls
electric mixer
drinking glass
pot holders
spatula
cooling rack

1. Preheat the oven to 350 degrees. Cover the baking sheets with parchment paper.

2. Make the cookies first. Cream the butter and sugar in a large bowl. Add the egg and vanilla. Mix until smooth.

3. Put the flour, salt, and baking powder in a small bowl. Stir. Add the flour mixture to the sugar mixture. Beat with the electric mixer. Mix in the sprinkles.

4. Roll the dough into 1-inch (2.5 cm) balls. Place them on the baking sheets. Flatten them with the bottom of the drinking glass.

5. Bake for 10 minutes. Put the cookies on a cooling rack. Let them cool completely.

6. Mix the frosting ingredients together in a small bowl. Spread frosting on the bottom of a cookie. Put another cookie on top to make a sandwich. Repeat with the rest of the cookies.

buttery
tea
cakes

MAKES 36 COOKIES

## INGREDIENTS

- 1 cup butter
- 1 teaspoon vanilla extract
- 2 cups powdered sugar
- 2 cups all-purpose flour
- 1 cup chopped walnuts
- 1/8 teaspoon ground cinnamon

## TOOLS

- baking sheets
- parchment paper
- measuring cups
- measuring spoons
- mixing bowls
- electric mixer
- pot holders
- spatula
- cooling rack
- spoon

1. Preheat the oven to 350 degrees. Cover the baking sheets with parchment paper.

2. Cream the butter in a large bowl. Mix in the vanilla and 1/2 cup powdered sugar. Add the flour and nuts. Mix well.

3. Refrigerate the dough for 30 minutes.

4. Roll the dough into 1-inch (2.5 cm) balls. Put the balls on the baking sheets. Space them 2 inches (5 cm) apart. Bake for 18 minutes or until they are light brown. Put the cookies on a cooling rack. Let them cool for 5 minutes.

5. Put the cinnamon and remaining powdered sugar in a small bowl. Stir. Coat the warm cookies with the sugar.

stained
glass
cookies

MAKES 36 COOKIES

## INGREDIENTS

- 1 bag hard candy
- 3 cups all-purpose flour
- 2 teaspoons ground ginger
- 1 teaspoon ground cinnamon
- 1 teaspoon baking soda
- ½ teaspoon nutmeg
- ¼ teaspoon salt
- ¾ cup butter
- ¾ cup white sugar
- ¾ cup molasses
- 1 egg
- 1 teaspoon vanilla extract

## TOOLS

- plastic zipper bags
- hammer
- measuring cups
- measuring spoons
- mixing bowls
- electric mixer
- plastic wrap
- baking sheets
- parchment paper
- rolling pin
- cutting board
- small and large heart shaped cookie cutters
- pot holders

1. Organize the hard candy by color. Put each color in a different plastic bag.
2. Crush the candy with a hammer.
3. Put the flour, ginger, cinnamon, baking soda, nutmeg, and salt in a medium bowl. Mix with an electric mixer.
4. Cream the butter and sugar in a large mixing bowl. Then stir in the molasses, egg, and vanilla.

### TIP

As you crush the candy, the pieces might poke holes in the bag. If this happens, place a **towel** around the bag. Then keep crushing!

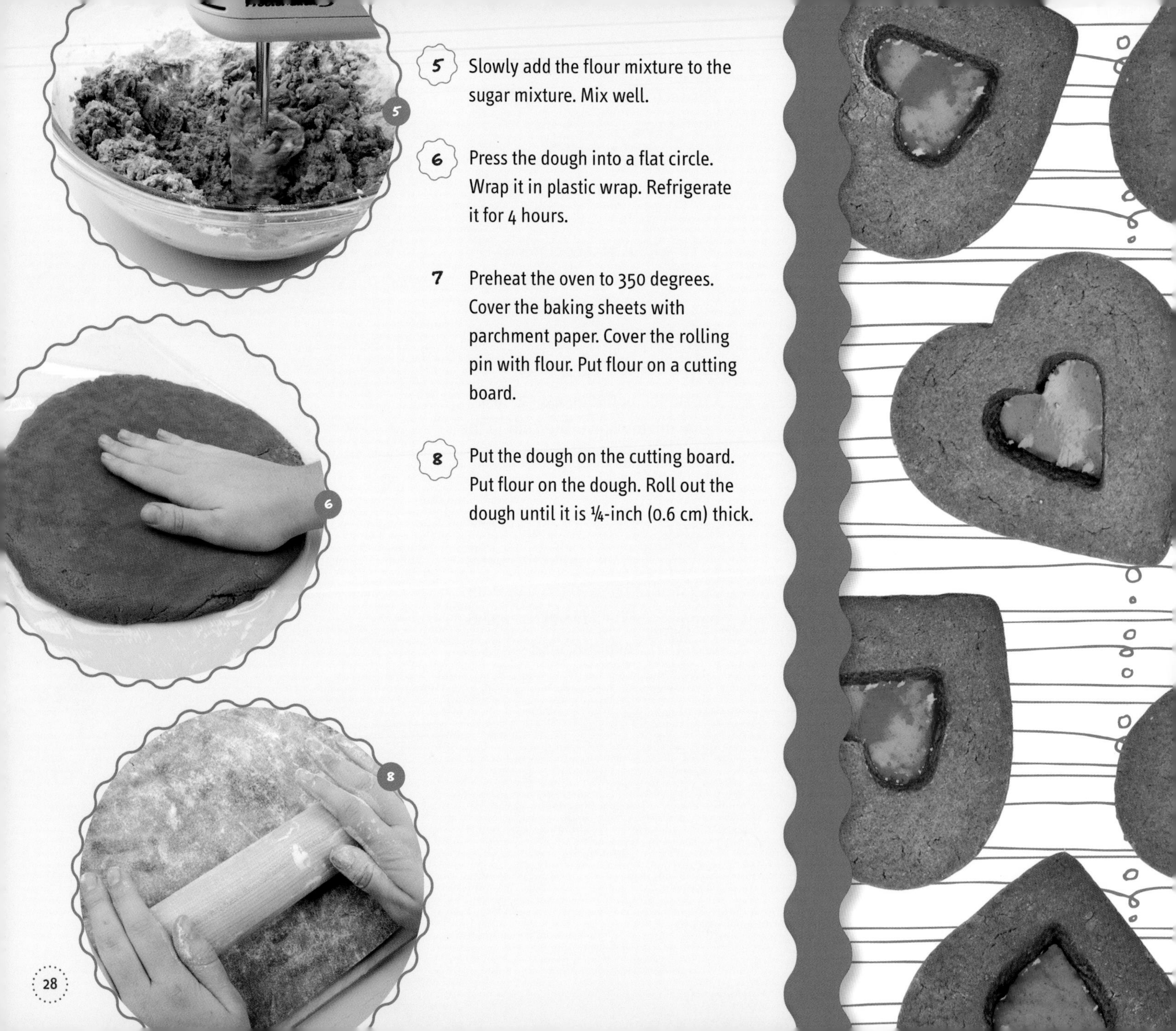


5 Slowly add the flour mixture to the sugar mixture. Mix well.

6 Press the dough into a flat circle. Wrap it in plastic wrap. Refrigerate it for 4 hours.

7 Preheat the oven to 350 degrees. Cover the baking sheets with parchment paper. Cover the rolling pin with flour. Put flour on a cutting board.

8 Put the dough on the cutting board. Put flour on the dough. Roll out the dough until it is ¼-inch (0.6 cm) thick.

9 Cut out cookies with the large cookie cutter.

10 Press the small cookie cutter in the center of each cookie. Remove the shape from the center.

11 Put the cookies on the baking sheets. Bake for 8 minutes or until they are light brown. Take them out of the oven.

12 Fill the center of each cookie with crushed candy. Bake for 3 minutes. Take out the cookies. Let them cool on the baking sheets.

red velvet delights

MAKES 24 COOKIES

## Ingredients

- 1 18-ounce box red velvet cake mix
- ½ cup vegetable oil
- 2 eggs
- 1 teaspoon baking powder
- 1 teaspoon vanilla extract
- 1½ cups white chocolate chips

## Tools

- baking sheets
- parchment paper
- measuring cups
- measuring spoons
- mixing bowls
- electric mixer
- mixing spoon
- pot holders
- spatula
- cooling rack

1. Preheat the oven to 350 degrees. Cover the baking sheets with parchment paper.
2. Put the cake mix, oil, eggs, baking powder, and vanilla in a large bowl. Mix with the electric mixer.
3. Add 1 cup white chocolate chips. Stir.
4. Put the dough 1 tablespoon at a time on the baking sheets.
5. Press the remaining chips on top of the cookies.
6. Bake for 10 minutes. Put the cookies on a cooling rack.

# GLOSSARY

amaze – to surprise or fill with wonder.

container – something that other things can be put into.

counter – a level surface where food is made.

delicious – very pleasing to taste or smell.

divide – to separate into equal groups or parts.

fluffy – light, soft, and airy.

layer – one thickness of something that may be over or under another thickness.

permission – when a person in charge says it is okay to do something.

recipe – instructions for making something.

slice – a thin piece cut from something.

towel – a cloth or paper used for cleaning or drying.

unique – different, unusual, or special.

utensil – a tool used to prepare or eat food.